A Piece of Perfection

A PIECE OF PERFECTION
by
Gwyndolin Gorg

Photographs
by
Gentry Gorg , Sunny Gorg

ISBN 979-8-218-14761-7

GOGAT PUBLISHING
67-1197 Mamalahoa Hwy. #2858
Waimea, Hawaii 96743'
Phone (808)885-2103

A Piece of Perfection

OFFERINGS

THE NATURAL LIVING WORLD

EARLY IN THE MORNING

early in the morn
the deep indigo star-filled sky has vanished
gold ... amber ... salmon colors
enveloping the space as sunrise appears
I awaken into an acceptance of the first light
release from the nights slumber
let go the covers of security and comfort

early in the morn
as I await the sky's bright blue return
an invisible force quietly dissipates
grey ... gliding ...shape-shifting cumulus clouds
on their way to distances near and far
as I ponder the unknown

early in the morn
multicolored flowers release fragrances
wafting through environments
sparkling flora blanketing the landscape
absorbing blessings of continuity
giving homage to creation

early in the morn
melodically chattering winged ones
sharing aural vibrations
harmonizing ... soothing nature's directions
declaring a new day's offering

early in the morn
a time that has never unfolded before
inhaling new day's promises
I prepare for fresh adventures
tentative offerings
stimulating ... captivating ... energizing
as sweet purity overrides my senses

NIGHT BLOOMING JASMINE

night blooming jasmine
land-based sea of magnificently … unexplainable sensations
overpowering logic
every cell of my existence filled with aromatic perfection
this momentary indulgence
in a matrix of completion

a gratifying frozen delight
flashes of contemplation reminding me of
the preciousness of what exists
becoming one with this encompassing fragrance
as sweet- smelling blossoms … prevailing wind currents
gently override any stagnation with scented purity

nothing else matters
my body is kissed in a pool of perfumed bliss
surrendering to the acceptance
listening to nocturnal creatures chanting
observing the night sky's heavenly glistening bodies
stars dancing … asteroids streaking

night blooming jasmine
lungs inhaling … lungs exhaling this radiance
pure delight
unwanted particles vanish
only the beauty remains

night blooming jasmine
lovely … lovely … lovely
teasing the senses … offering wonder
in a valley of scented filled revelry
while perfuming the darkness
in harmonious receptivity

NIGHT REFLECTION

light fades away
glowing ... flickering bodies
streaming across the heavens
illuminating the sky

the waning moon's last phase
of its inevitable cycle as it revolves
away from the sun revealing a vast
heaven of endless constellations
constantly evolving mysteries
telepathically broadcasting

magnificently adorned owl gracefully takes stage
silently gliding over the terrain
without its signature call
where only one's thoughts are heard

nature's unseen creatures
crawling in and out of crevices
aware of the tasty morsels they provide
gently fade into quietness

eastwardly light awaits
curtain of darkness to lift
its predetermined appearance
making visible the illusion of newness
evoking questions of the infinite

a desire for oneness
stirs the earth's sleeping inhabitants
as biorhythms titillate the senses
a reminder of the ever-repeating cycle
of a quest for a gratifying conclusion

AN HOMAGE TO TREES

majestically tall trees dwarfing their environment
appearing taller than forever
reaching beyond a translucent cloud cover
howling winds waltzing into oblivion
exhaling in the stratosphere
overshadowing meandering streams
winding and flowing to the next tributary

trees regal… trees small
supported by root systems
clinging to stable … unstable anchors
teetering on the fringes of existence

deforestation
heavy footprints uprooting … uprooting
closer living-to-the-ground creatures
scurrying to places of freedom
four-legged ones trapped
ear shattering … shrill sounding chainsaws
disturbing the calm
petroleum saturated earth
rotting foliage … fallen nests with unhatched eggs
disappearing habitats
seen … unseen

clear cut trees for cities big and buildings tall
destructive human forces
replace foliage for emotional greed
trees decimated to windblown dust
forest supreme vanishes like a dream
a reality where pollination will decrease
an actuality where oxygen can cease

trees … trees
magnificent citadels   suppliers of life's essence
trees … with gratitude I humble myself to you

A NATURAL OBSERVATION

Singing birds telegraphing beautiful sounds
across the threshold of ever-expanding loveliness
where joy calls
brightly lit path with luminous vibrations
summoning the core of all good

basking sunflowers … aromatic gardenias
low-hanging wisteria … indescribable flora
honoring their origins
overpowering the ordinary
accenting the environment
catapulting the senses into a place
of torrential reverence

redwoods … sequoias stretching
to unimaginable heights
remaining anchored to a force
delivering radiance to those
who can accept an undefined excellence
while continuing their trek

jacarandas releasing their signature petals
laying delicate carpets of lavender flowers
gently perfuming their surroundings
giving pause to onlookers
whose exhalation releases uncluttered acceptance

green reigning … thriving cacti on a treeless desert floor
where a reduction of moisture
evaporating precipitation takes control
succulent's shriveling brilliance
morph into indefinable matter
becoming one with thirsty … hardened earthen clay
vanishing into a yesterday's memory

HURRICANE

hurricane coming
whispering winds asking
are you prepared…are you prepared
rain falling … fierce … murmuring breezes calling

sirens alarming
shrill ear- piercing repetitive octaves
people running for shelter
attempting to adapt
chaotic … unsteady gusts impair vision
red… green … yellow flashing lights

untethered force of a fast-moving squall
cutting its way through with surgical precision
indescribable cadence
roofs collapsing … boulders rolling
leaves twirling … branches bending
intensifying erratic sounds to nature 's cleanup
shelters beckoning would be victims in need of serenity

surf pounding upon shelled robbed seashores
adorned with litter from far away destinations
roaring … spiraling … bellowing winds
with increased volume
are you prepared … are you prepared

feeling afraid rushing about in confusion
shielding emotions
like boarded windows preventing destructive intrusions
uncontrollable tears showering down cheeks
like streams having lost their directions
adrift in a sea of uncertainty

searching for escape routes
clinging to a force
to keep from floating away becoming a distant memory

TREES

braced by an invisible force of the earth's rotation
trees deeply rooted … trees standing tall
roots anchored to unseen depths
strongly glued to a gravitational substance

intertwined branches
symmetrically clinging to limbs
swaying … snapping
bending … cracking
depositing vegetation
silently witnessing
the earth

holding answers to
the secrets of time
peaceful … strong … beautiful
meditators
the trees

ME .... TREES

walking alone on tree lined paths
leading to more of the same
continuation ... repetition
absolute stillness reminds me
each step an invitation into the silence
that only nature can hear
this solitude engulfing the surroundings
mantras released from feathered ones
sharing their continuous melodies
as pure sound pleasure
vibrating my aural receptors
I respectfully honor

my aloneness manifests an awareness
stepping lightly along well traveled paths
carved out by undomesticated four-legged ones
in this presence of peace ... tranquility abides
reminding me of my responsibilities
reminding me of my embedded footprint
I become more aware of unconscious disturbances

absorbing the radiance in this quietness
penetrating deeply into my being
vibrations emanating from the ethers
uninterrupted stillness enters into my private places
soundless acceptance where only the ME dwells
visions of clarity manifest ... solutions reveal themselves
trees in sturdy stance
some reaching to infinity ...
some bearing witness closer to the earth
newly realized freedom bursts forth
unrestrained happiness takes control
winds halt ... I freeze in the presence ...in the comfort ...
dwelling among magnificent meditators
the trees

IN A GARDEN

raindrops drench thirsty land
germinating seeds … transforming … bursting through …
clay-hardened …   sandy porous-rocky soil

newly emerging sprouts
sharing nature's magnificence

mother earth responds in acceptance
shimmering fallen leaves smile upwardly to the sun
displaying seasonal changes
supplying necessary life affirmations

freshly moistened earth welcoming
my naked feet
becoming one with wet rain-drenched soil
massaging the earth
over … under… around each of my toes
appreciating the connection to our mother
who satisfies … saturates our needs most preciously

A DAY

a dazzling new day
beauteous moments filling the atmosphere
brightness bursting through
unforeseen radiance projecting peace

melodiously pulsating day
nature's inhabitants chanting in unison
instinctual … unrehearsed … repetitive overtones
pacific winds releasing melodies like unrelenting harp strings

an unfolding mysterious day
presenting a uniqueness
similar but never duplicated
each experience displaying its own identity

gloriously celebratory day
experiencing the given victory …
eating from the tree of abundance …
leaping into that which offers gratifying adoration

unlike any other day
joyously brightly lit day
sun kissing the atmosphere
shape-shifting clouds
irrefutable reminders
of the immensity of the mysterious magic of the universe

MY WALK AT DUSK

the perfection of the natural order
permeates my being with incredulous radiance
a breath of reducing wonderment
as I question illusions

I breathe in the essences of the splendor
absorb the last radiance of a magnificently hued sunset
where mundane opinionated judgements lose their importance
in this Now
the relevant moment

the perfection of the natural order
overpowers my reasoning with harmonious reverence
a hushed acceptance
as I gently meander
into a
temporary experience
as those in preparation for a sunless journey
settle down to touch another realm

my walk at dusk alerts me to the elusive surroundings
as fluttering leaves surrender to a windless evening

reminding me of the mysterious immensity of the universe
reminding me of my smallness as I survey the sky
reminding me of the fading light that returns
reminding me of the necessity of peaceful participation
reminding me of the fulfillment within my reach

INTROSPECTION

MY FRUSTRATION

patience and forgiveness vanish
strenuously moving through the muck
grasping tightly
circling around myself in cyclonic rapidity
howling winds in my mind reveal an upturned unstable perception
an unfamiliar me losing hold of my beautiful nature
pulsating at an increased rate

breathing in … waves crashing the shore
breathing out … discarding debris

allowing the vibration of stillness to have its sway
activating reminders penetrating the surfaces
erasing stubbornness
elevating consciousness
recognizing the available goodness
focusing on thankfulness

remembering the immensity of choices
gradual dissolution of frustration
vanishing into the ethers
I began dancing lightly without a gravitational influence.

A LOST AND FOUND ME

searching for myself
in a forest of flying fowl
perched atop cloud touching trees
releasing their melodies

meandering through densely populated wooded areas
thorny berry bushes obstructing narrow paths
prickly intrusions like wild thoughts
preventing my forward flow

looking for myself
under a canopy of cloudless skies
with endlessly blended directions
free from gloom filled realities

a confused me with
heavily burdened thoughts
heavily placed feet
disturbing carpets of vegetation
whispering leaves blanketing the landscape
gently succumb to the earth's calling

continuing my search clutching myself
walking along … suspended
an unreal dream of yesterday's memories
sun rays streaking through branches
a boundless vitality of trees
reaching for the sun's blessings

pristine unhindered streams freely flowing
bordered in glimmers of a hopeful continuity
a newly realized me manifests as
pureness and promises of clarity
remind me of the need for self -trust

roaming NORTHWARD,
wandering SOUTHWARD
going EAST... moving WEST
each direction here I am

embracing a soul soothing solace
with wind cleansed visions
bringing rose petal fragrances
lavender memories ... jasmine delights
leading to harmonious reflections
brightening the way

vanishing obstructions
no escape from the real me
breathing in ... surrendering
surrendering ... surrendering
embracing myself
I embrace ME

EVOLVING REFLECTIONS

reflecting on the horrors ... the sorrows of this world
causes a heavy heart to shrivel into a dark place
from the prevailing negative fallout

reflecting on the pain that humans lodge against each other
venomous words ... hurtful actions ... dreadful thoughts
unconscious negative participation
permitting openings where shadows reside

reflecting on the darkness that leads
anger ...fear... confusion
without awareness of more life-affirming contrasts
guiding to smoother routes
revealing courses of brightness and clarity

reflecting on the magnificent possibilities' life reveals
sweetness...laughter and brighter horizons
oozing with delicate fragrances that encumber me
sweet continuity of the available radiance
illuming my forward direction

reflecting on
yesterday's lessons ... tomorrow's promises ...
the ever evolving now
walking through a field of unending vistas
releasing unwanted reminiscences
releasing unwanted reminiscences

A HEART'S LONGING

a heart's longing for that which is available to all
in the farewell kisses of the dimming light
another tomorrow offers
an awakened sunrise
possibilities of a new awareness
hopeful wishes that the stirrings
in my heart vibrate at a frequency inviting
love ... peace ... joy ... wisdom ...eternal blessings

CRAZY WINDS

bending boughs
snapping branches
whistling…screaming gusts
twisting … rotating squalls
soprano and bass tone winds
falling trees
shattering barriers
obstructing clear pathways
uprooting my calm
fear steps forward claiming my sense of self
clouding my vision
creating a mind's haze

howling … fiercely … rapidly moving gales
uprooting gnarled tree roots
clutching onto myself
wishing for a liberator
looking for shelter
a directionless search
fear-filled fuse attempting to ignite
an explosion in my head
twisting and twirling me about
my inner voice cries out… hold on

anchoring myself tightly
releasing uncertainty
disrupting winds reluctantly move on
escorting away my imbalance
brighter vision erupts
golden hued leaves
share their layers of magnificence

HOW DO I

how do I explain unfamiliar unwelcome intrusions
sometimes invading my understanding of who I am
heart palpitations …raised brows … agitated entrails
feelings beyond the reasonable

how do I continuously access that illumination
which washes away gloom … negative thought forms
saturating the mind stream
causing fear … anger … uncertainty
lest I be blown into untraveled areas awaiting discovery
where all seems to be floating in a sea of wonder

how do I remain afloat on this journey of mine
big waves enveloping the shoreline
holding on for flawless directions
riding the wind currents … grasping tightly
unexplainable … unexplored … glittering perplexity
patience beyond mundane obviousness
each new moment
revealing newly discovered focuses
awaiting resolutions

BITS OF ME

motionless shadows lurking in all directions
blocking my luminosity
my outer and my inner
clutching … releasing
inhaling … exhaling
my fortitude weakens
quiet voice in my head repeatedly echoing
brighten your light
brighten your light
brighten your light

fragments of me scattering about
gasping … grasping
searching for a clear path
vibrating … gyrating … pulsating shadows of my mind
blocking my brilliance

quiet voice echoing in my head
intensify your light … intensify your light
pieces of me reunite … bits of myself reunite
dissipating … weakening…powerless
shadows of my mind are put to rest
satisfied quiet voice smiles
all of myself proclaims victory
all of me manifests completely

MY CONFUSION

discordant winds blowing an invisible force
upsetting the natural balance

reminding me of what has been
delicate journey into questionable realms
offering solutions too difficult to interpret

a quickening in my gut magnifying my confusion
while dwarfing the reasonable
producing an unending quest for answers

in the midst of it all

I ask
why... who... when... what

A LIFE EXPERIENCE

Life envelops and assesses my every direction
penetrating the atmospheres
doubt … confusion … sadness … fearful intrusions
invite vulnerability
tightly grasping
a thinning protective armor
searching for
strength … courage …clarity
amongst the bumps and ruts
.

whisking away fearful insinuations
allowing nurturing breezes' embrace
to provide forgotten relief
where
the road bends
the unending
mourner's tales are hurled away

traversing the road of life
grabbing hold … caressing myself

cerebral blockages
dissolve away … transform into
stale … forgotten memories
saluting my authentic inclinations
accessing virtuous regions

lucidity and understanding
reveal beautifully paved probabilities

disassembling hindrances
lodged in the hollows of my understanding
reinforcing my stamina … unrestrained authority
secure satisfaction
a welcomed frequency

SOLITUDE

in my solitude
interminable concerns spring forth
I ponder the sacred geometrical
magnificence of life's intricate designs
manifesting in plants … animals …minerals
perfectly patterned natural balance

in my solitude … limitless possibilities
floating through my senses as
I attempt to light a flame
igniting a cognitive awareness
displaying an acknowledgement

in my solitude … solutions give rise to
endless timeless cycles of uncertainty
waves of an energetic flow
release on to the shores of my understanding

in my solitude … tears once remembered have
dissipated into infinite steams
cleansing stagnation … allowing an opening
clogged unremitting channels
once again flow

in my solitude … fresh visions catapult
into unfamiliar domains
awaiting acceptance
where illuminated paths
offer magnified reflections

MY REGENERATION

movement of bamboo dancing to vibrations of the breeze
emanating a continuous sound mantra
pristine environment
at the edge of a pool disquieted
by an unyielding rainbow hued waterfall
searching more deeply for me
we have a commitment … my ego self and me
releasing a punctured ego
interrupting the natural surge of
insensitive yearnings … unconscious receptivity
which created a limiting paradigm
giving permission to fear and anger

infinite blue skies temporarily
obstructed by moisture … laden… drifting clouds
depositing a soothing precipitation
a momentary cleansing
cooling … calming my agitation
rejecting my accepted stagnation

reluctantly surrendering from a lack of certainty
willing to envelop that which needs nurturing
my realization awakens to promises
where clarity is my choice
obstacles preventing my free flow dissolve

becoming immersed in a magnificent essence
my spirit soars to mysterious regions
too stunning for human cognition
my hearts special connection is
receptive to receive the good that is available

a flawed ego yields as the east winds blow away haziness
I hold onto Me and walk upright on the path to
my regeneration

WITHIN THE CONFINES OF MY CAPACITY

within the confines of my capacity
I attempt to control my eroding … destructive thoughts
before they degenerate into pools of misunderstanding
giving rise to uncertainty where a misstep might cause me to shrivel

within the confines of my capacity
I attempt to balance my comprehension
before incredulous confusion envelops my being
where a longing for awareness awaits my receptivity

within the confines of my capacity
I attempt to gain entry into newer understandings
before a cognitive cloudburst obstructs my clarity
corrals my vision … disseminates sparks of curiosity

within the confines of my capacity
I attempt to elevate my awareness
where a semblance of unexplored possibilities guides me
to a newly found radiance with glowing prisms

before dark shadows become too profound
I attempt to raise my consciousness beyond the ordinary
seize fresh perceptions for more tranquil horizons
as I survey within the confines of my capacity

WAITING IN THE WINGS OF LIFE

waiting in the wings of life
the outskirts of fulfillment
a welcoming call as life's curtain opens
taking stage as a newly arrived one
wobbly...insecure venturing out of my comfort
questioning my participation
reluctantly becoming enveloped
as scenes change

in my private soliloquy
attempting to attract new illusions
craving freedom like a soaring eagle
from dark obscurations to a shimmering new intensity
disavowing fear-based manifestations

stepping forward on life's stage rejecting a profane reality
permitting an illuminated sub-text to manifest
where a virginal alertness upstages the mundane
stepping down center... unwelcoming shadows wane

acknowledging my newly revealed glow
flickering uncertainty subsides
releasing a first-time brilliance
giving purpose to that which seems remote

the curtain of life opens wider
I bow in acceptance of a new awareness

CHANGES IN MY PERCEPTION

as if summoned by a force that offers no apologies
where the now and the forever
remain attached to sunlight's radiance

impenetrable mental mounds
that have appeared motionless
ineffable thunderous mind storms
clamor to
uproot my authenticity

summer's sun bursting through the inertia
perceived blockages
burning … chiseling … away into oblivion
lingering daylight … projecting brightness
fluctuating observations
magnetized receptors pause in readiness

autumn breezes dispel doubt … appearances that dismay
left by confused memories
a dissolving mist covering my longing for clarity
realigning my senses
alerting me to promises of unexplored horizons

red leaves … gold leaves drop to the earth
offering a chance of renewal
blowing winds awaiting my agreement
whisking away adulterated possibilities
non-essentials tightly clinging
to my consciousness…. hindering my perception

changes in my awareness
accepting the brightness that is mine
evolving …transforming
a more expanded sensibility
the dance of forever leaping into unexplained luminosity

THE UNFURLING

at daybreak … transitioning heavenly bodies of the night sky
give the illusion of finality
critters re-emerging from places of escape
golden crowned… red winged roosters
alert the populace with timeless alarms
agitate some two-legged ones
releasing expletives

at daybreak lying in bed absorbing the radiance of freshness
satisfying temperatures encumbering my being
amber colored sunrise soothes my vision
continuous salt infused breezes waft through
fluttering translucent curtains donning my windows
neighborly aromas pierce my surrounding
with their succulent offerings

at daybreak … realigning myself for what lies ahead
inhaling the possibility of brighter moments
where manifestations become realized

at daybreak … opening up to the promise of newness
the apex of stillness wanes
daily vibrations emerge
a new dawning excites my being

at daybreak … welcoming the sun's rays with jubilant enthusiasm
satisfying my curiosity with wonder
my senses become heightened
with promises of virtual experiences

at daybreak … breathing into a new me
the physical me exhales the excesses
the spiritual me inhales the mystery
the joyful me jumps and laughs and sings
adorning myself in the essence of the magnificence

UNADULTERATED BLISS

grasping hold of me
in my quiet reflections
appreciating the magnificent unfolding
endlessly available as I quiet my wanting's

mother nature's beauty in all its offerings
vibrating harmonies as the wind rustles
eternal rhythm of the waves ebbing and flowing
undulating joy fills my being
words become insignificant
credulous probabilities
an awakened consciousness
awaiting openings to display luminosity

sorrowful songs dissipate
as sun and raindrops produce rainbows
reflecting inspiring glory

absorbing the goodness that is forever present
becoming one with all
light radiates from my words … deeds … thoughts
obscuring shadows that block my sparkle
releasing sparks that may ignite
an undefinable relationship

morning sun radiates my sense of me
evening sun glows in my awareness
affirming a connection
with the infinite invisible force that governs all
I dance … I leap into boundless spaces
where prevailing truth … laughter … joy
transport me into a blanket of
pure unadulterated bliss

WHAT IS PERFECTION?

Is it a mother duckling
Escorting her progeny to a first swim

OR
Abating bird chirps as the sky goes dim

OR
A full belly un -desirous of more

AS
Laughter and joy escape through a door

IS IT
Children giggling together as they play
Catching the sun's brilliance, the first of may

COULD IT BE
The petals we smell with fragrances sweet

OR
Lovers with eye contact as they meet

MAYBE IT IS
Chlorophyll that makes the grasses grow green

OR
jungles and ravines never before seen

POSSIBLY
Feet dangling in a gently moving stream
Embracing sweet memories from a dream

OR
Negative ions as we deeply breathe in
Insuring good health with all our kin

MAYBE
Walking in a forest where trees grow tall
Listening to oneself while heeding the call

COULD IT BE
The steady movement of a gentle breeze
Cleansing environments where some will sneeze

OR
Lustrous sunny days with temperatures sweet
Ingesting cacao a tropical sweet

MAYBE
It is quietness that signals the call

OR
Life's pure resplendence and that is all

NO BEGINNING NO ENDING

NO BEGINNING
NO BEGINNING
NO ENDING
NO ENDING
NO ENDING
NO ENDING
NO BEGINNING
NO BEGINNING NO BEGINNING
NO ENDING
NO ENDING
NO ENDING NO BEGINNING NO BEGINNING
NO BEGINNING and on and on and on and on and on and on
and on and on and on and on and on and on and on and on and

etcetera … etcetera… etcetera… etcetera… etcetera
NO ENDING

VIBRATIONS

fear ... anger ... avarice
dominating... pulsating ... agitating
inwardly ... outwardly
hurt manifests ... uughh...

blame.... sadness ... tears ... guilt
anticipating ... regurgitating ... tolerating
inwardly ... outwardly
pain manifests ... ow

love ... forgiveness ... patience ... kindness
meditating ... communicating ... appreciating
inwardly ... outwardly
tranquility ... manifests
ah ... ah... ah...

THE MASTER OF ME

what is the purpose of my life …

To be in perfect harmony with my incredible self
synchronized with an invisible force everywhere present
…
allowing no uncharted distractions to take control
opening to broader perceptions

forgiving self … forgiving others
renewing my reality
altering my trajectory
transforming from the disquieted life
where my unconsciousness gave power
… to a self-righteous ego …
… permitting fear to override my reasoning …

… what is the purpose of my life …

breathing in…. breathing out
awakening to more awareness
linking a
stronger realignment with my spirit connected
DNA
breathing in …. breathing out
etching
peace… harmony… blissful health… love… balance …patience
into my psyche
new priorities
override my thoughts… words… deeds
I become the master of ME

THE BLOSSOMING NEW DAY

in the blossoming hour of the day
sleep slowly releases its hold
roosters signal the emergence of a sunrise unfolding
I leap into my consciousness
discarding shackles of slumber

in the dawning of the new day
pristine perfection glistens
where dew flavors its surroundings
I brace myself in the a. m.
breathing in an overpowering freshness

in the mornings early luminous light
I prepare for the goodness that prevails
discard temptations that
limit my evolvement

in the fullness of a new day
I envision the unfolding of eternal peace
my acceptance summons brighter beginnings

THE LIGHT ALWAYS RETURNS

even when darkness appears … light returns
easiness … acceptance of delight awaits the discoverer
shadows present illusions causing a loss of footing
while searching for new directions that lead to clarity

charged particles ignite sensations attempting to escape
into the abyss … into the land of darkness
where shimmers of light appear remote
beyond the land of obscurity where birds serenade

a desire for ease springs forth
blowing winds clearing paths
perfectly placed foot- steps
away from false illusions
fragrant blossoms perfuming their surroundings
sparks of loveliness for those who can accept

summoned by the incomprehensible
no escape from that which illumes the way
illusions of a lack of luminosity create alienation
from the glimmer that cannot be blocked out
imagined gloom dissipates …particles scatter … muddled fragments vanish
the heart's heaviness is released
rediscovering the glow
illuming … radiating a forward path
a brilliance bathes the atmosphere with visions of clarity

even when darkness appears … light returns

REMEMBERING

into the timeless realms of my existence
where the infinite resides
an overview of newly discovered possibilities
as time collides into an unexplainable brilliance
illumining the passageway for vistas unknown

lost in the search for the meaning of the eternal
awaiting incoming revelations
where a continuity of self-redefines itself
I search for answers as winds pluck
the strings of the universe connecting
to melodies that transport me beyond the reasonable
to uncluttered scenarios where no chaos resides

walking … skipping … whirling in circles
tiptoeing on the surface of my true self
with a delicate connection
in the direction of the unspoken chants
I remember… I remember
to embrace my beautiful essence
that resides within
I remember… I remember

FREQUENCIES

listening… not with ears …
looking … not with eyes
touching…not with hands
sensing frequencies
exploring
mysterious sparkles
of unexplored awareness

continuously accessing that spark
breathing myself clean
dissolving clinging uninvited attachments
hanging on the margins of my consciousness

blessed undistorted acceptance
vanishing gloom
wonderous sensations traversing light
offering a sweet path
disintegrating heavy imprints
blocking accessible brightness

on this life journey
newness constantly revealed
recognizing the immensity this limitless creation
living for joyous moments
new adventures … regeneration
walking into the next frequency

TENDERNESS

THE DAY'S CURTAIN

the day's curtain has closed
songbird's chatter has quieted
lovers holding hands sauntering about
as fragrances sweet overpower the ordinary
flickering stars
from distances
beyond imaginations … beyond horizons
reminders of the sky's immensity

lovers committing to unending promises that
keep each anchored to the other
irrational changes generated by each touch
electrifying the senses …igniting currents
teasing
tempting
pleasing
until sunrise again appears

THE BREAKUP

you rejected me
as the shadows overtook
the bright blue hues of our tomorrows

you ejected me from your life
integrity vanished with the day's dimming
treachery became more powerful than lucidity
clear of paths we once tread collapsed

you discarded me …I discarded you
painful sorrows we were cast me into
decaying blossoms fell to the ground
uninterrupted tears rapidly flowing
down as torrents

the suffering we lodged on each other
lost ourselves as our egotistical perceptions
morphed into fields of withering flowers

yelling out in disbelief
solutions had taken flight
awaiting …. newness
decelerating deeper and deeper
into the depths of self-pity

awaiting a new sunrise
shackles of confusion loosened
releasing me from bondage
a newborn awareness sprung forth
self-love emerged
setting me free to run
in a field of multicolored
sweetness

WILL YOU STILL LOVE ME

when the sparkling stars are obscured by the brightness of the moon
my reasoning becomes obscured by the shadows of my mind
dark clouds block the sunshine
the sweetness of the mango becomes bitter
my laughter turns to scorn

WILL YOU STILL LOVE ME
my smoothness shrivels
like fresh grapes exposed to the sun...becoming raisins
when moisture dissipates
… wrinkles appear
the newness of today fades away
tomorrow is far in the distance
rainbows lose their brilliance
bitterness minimizes the sweetness

WILL YOU STILL LOVE ME
when my steps are as slow as the flow of cold molasses
my confusion obscures my clarity
storms in my mind uproot the grey matter
my cognition takes an extended vacation
when my need for assistance becomes a 24-7 priority

WILL YOU STILL LOVE ME
WILL YOU STILL LOVE ME
WILL YOU STILL LOVE ME
WILL YOU STILL LOVE ME
WILL   I   STILL LOVE ME

LOVERS

lovers holding hands
strolling on petunia bordered paths
lit by flickering stars emitting light
from distant universes with horizons
beyond the imagination of what is evident
the day's curtain has closed
love birds chatter has quieted

lovers surrendering to their desires
as hormonal signals alert the senses
transmitting guttural volcanic eruptions
crumbling knees and shared emotions
warm the heart unite the souls

lovers sharing eternal promises
anchor themselves to each other
where incredulous changes
generated by each touch
send energetic currents
titillate the senses
as the night surrenders to a new dawn

LOVERS AT THE SEA

impetuous lovers run into the sea
he's ... chasing her
she's ... giggling with delight
two bodies
entwined into a rollicking frenzy
effervescent whitecaps
wash away a conjugal longing
impede a passion
as turtles float by

MY HEART

my heart igniting flames
burning away cold … dreary
blankets of an icy-covered consciousness
blocked by frozen ideas
when clarity takes a detour

my heart appreciating nature's offerings
songbirds echoing melodies
waterfalls surging …roaring
emptying into crystal clear pools
purple morning glories
dangling … climbing … releasing loveliness

my heart swelling with delight
a joyful expanse filling my acceptance
gliding into indefinable realms
steadying my balance
grasping imaginary filaments
suspended from the heavens

my heart glistening with pristine awareness
responding to the amazement
within easy access
bright sparks blocking gloom
illuminating a path where murky imprints
leave no impression

my heart succumbing to radiant life-affirming sensations
words becoming insignificant

feelings beyond the reasonable
steady rhythms harmonizing
with the earth's resonance
the unexplainable magnificence my soul is heir to
my heart surrendering as we embrace

my lover and I
floating through the heavens
leaving no impression
an absence of gravitational encumbrances

this blessed life-journey
the immensity of this limitless creation
each twinkling offering new adventures
walking into the next

WHEN I LOOK AT YOU MY HEART SINGS

when I look at you
my heart sweetly serenades my being with melodious vibrations
transporting me into unexplored regions

when I hear your voice
my senses give way to unimaginable longings
escorting me to gratifying sensations

when I touch you
my cells express divine connections
creating unparalleled emotions

when I walk with you
my focused gait anchors me
contemplating depths beyond the imagination

when I think of you
my soul pirouettes in imaginary realms
dancing and floating devoid of gravity

when I am with you
my joy overpowers all doubt
reverberating a universal contentment

as joy... forgiveness ... patience ...tenacity ... integrity
envelops our understanding
our love becomes magnified

A REAWAKENED KISS

the kiss ... the touch
rekindling lost forgotten feelings
agitating and stirring emotions
with my new realized acceptance
that cries out for joyous bliss

the kiss ... the touch
removes me from a finite realm
guiding me to an accessible place
revealing hidden desires
creating volcanic stirrings
signaling a sensory explosion

the kiss ... the touch
re-awakens aroused sensations
my body relaxes into acceptance
reducing an inner longing
that might erupt into a fire
that burns out of control

oh the kiss ...oh the sweet touch

FEMALES

I GET TO BE ME

I get to be me,
browned-skinned beauty,
coffee colored skin ...two drops of coconut cream
sweet caramel and a touch of heat
offering a warm heart open to all

I get to be me
full lips saturate a receiver
leaving indelible memories
too breathtaking to erase
lips creating eternal smiles
sealed into one's consciousness

I get to be me
perfectly formed soft round
upstanding mouth-perfect breast
facing the sky
perky nipples perched in readiness
as hormones momentarily burp

I get to be me
rounded derriere perfectly protruding
vibrating sensually with each motion
giving pleasure to onlookers
who feign disinterest
but smile in secret

I get to be me
a lover of humanity
with a forgiving spirit
evolving in life affirming directions
accepting and rejecting and growing
and giving thanks for the me that I get to be

LOVELY WOMAN

lovely woman
slumbering in the radiance of bark less eucalyptus trees
stretching above their canopy
into an unreachable lapis colored sky
singing songs of grace
for you and for me

lovely woman
in meditative posture
inhaling the radiance of freshly turned earth
as four legged ones with poised antlers
pause in readiness
as an unexpected vibration
sends them leaping away

lovely woman
searching for stillness and calm
with controlled inhalation and exhalation
as pollinating bees flutter from blossom to blossom
perpetuating continuity in their dance of joy
multicolored flowers glisten in acceptance

lovely woman
surrendering to the elements
with erect posture and outstretched palms
as the crawling ones tunnel through
softly upturned terrain

lovely woman
connecting with the earth
enveloped in a perfect breeze
as perfection becomes more than a thought
brown … yellow … green leaves fall to the earth
offering their gifts for a more fertile tomorrow

lovely woman
accepting the present moments
adorned with grey colored locks
lavender and lilac attire
humming praises of joy
while receiving the blessings of
never before possibilities

lovely woman
melding into an enveloping reverence
an awakened consciousness transports a desirous one
into endless dances of forever
where the ambiance of perfection prevails.

ANGRY WOMAN

cyclonic thoughts
negatively vibrating
with hummingbird velocity
moving with indefinable speed
permitting pointed dagger like speech
to overtake the hidden beauty
that lies beneath the cell wall

Angry Woman
pulsating with strident energy
distancing all in her path
woeful verbiage
shaking acceptable norms
from their foundations

Angry woman
accepting egotistical dictates
limiting the availability of self-growth
lost in a sea of blame
where the ebb and flow of the tides halt
pushing away a possible life raft
offering a contrasting perspective
awaiting a savior to make life sweet

Angry woman
giving her power away to self-pity
crying inside unable to allow
vulnerability to surface
discovery of the real person
might be too revealing

Angry woman
embracing a private inner fear
on a journey of confusion
plotting an escape to realms far away
where only she resides

UNIVERSAL WOMAN

picked cotton ... spun thread ... made kimchi
harvested rice... prepared collards...tortillas... tofu
carried drinking water from free-flowing rivers
washed the garments ... dried them on the rocks
In view of rough-skinned ... hungry ... wide-eyed crocks

UNIVERSAL WOMAN
senselessly mutilated with indescribable pain
cared unselfishly for the baby in her womb
sold the girls at sunrise for the family to survive
secretly cried washed away the preordained guilt
pondered the question why her life was so built

UNIVERSAL WOMAN
seduced by those obsessed with confusion and lust
previous victim accepting her power
allowing her true essence now to flower
able to forgive... releasing the pain she was lent
thunderous histories make their final descent

UNIVERSAL WOMAN
crying at times ... expressing vulnerability
encouraging others when she can
offering love.... but with a firm hand
fabulous woman... not giving in to fear
laughing... always spreading good cheer

UNIVERSAL WOMAN
directing and taking control when she must
sharing with world-class leaders that which is just
singing songs of freedom … for justice and peace
jetting to faraway places previously unknown

envisioning an unblemished utopia called home

UNIVERSAL WOMAN
absorbed in dreams of life's enduring mysteries
letting go the illusion … remembering all is transitory
discarding life's heavy weights

breathing in and out

no one completes her… she is already complete

The Universal Woman… totally…totally …replete

ABUSE

VOICELESS VICTIM AT A COCKTAIL PARTY

in a dimly lit corner... I stand
your invasion into my solitude ... my tranquility
a regurgitation of incessant words
aggressively dominating conversation
solution-less chatter
repetitive outpourings
attempting to inflate a voluminous ego
lacking melodious syncopation
no escape for me
captured in my politeness

tediously inappropriate words... more words
your endless one direction verbiage
flows like a downhill stream
opinions and more opinions
ego-driven definitions
a communication cavity
I feel pushed to the edge
no opportunity am I given to share a thought

my personal space assaulted
pounding sensations in my head
well-bred ... appropriate posture ...patience
prevent me from shouting
...
a momentary breath
I take a drink from a crystal flute
resume listening
as words and more words persist

THE RAPE

he saw the butt
ignored her plea
outrageous selfishness
gave him a glee

he saw the breast
was unable to see
the decent man
that he could be

he saw the lips
she attempted to flee
numb was his heart
a bully ... an abuser was he

expelled was his brain
ignored her pain
horrible horror
consciousness slain

soiled was her body
not in the plan
was it testosterone
that guided the man

she was his object
a treatment unjust
a fractured aggressor
who surrendered to lust

his pain was not the reason
he made a choice to commit treason
selfishness... incompleteness
was what he had chosen
human empathy completely frozen

BOY'S INNOCENCE STOLEN

my male identifier stood erect
unfamiliar sensations overpowered me
an unwelcomed aggression
forced me into submission
confused acceptance and rejection
paved the way for new vibrations

fondling and kissing
took control of my objectivity
pushed me into surrender '
secretly laughing and crying
unwanted feelings crept into
my consciousness

touching and sucking
overpowered my sense of honor
trapped me into a penitentiary of
endless agitation and forced tolerance
as sacrificed hormones gave way
to new unexplored guilt stirring feelings

hormones awry
unsolicited vocal changes
overpowering my control
conflicted desire … physicalized
confusion becomes more prevalent

my young self
lost for a while in lustful agitation
guilt … confusion
kisses … more fondling … and more
the male identifier relaxes
I question my involvement

BULLIED

forced into my inner origin
of continuance
with brutality
harsh … breathy … unsteady rhythm
pinned down in a prison of pain
powerless vulnerability
as I unwillingly surrender
to a
temporary clitoral pleasurable sensation
with confusing acceptance
as
two unbridled souls merge
followed by my overpowering
guilt
anger
downward eyes
repetitious occurrences produce loved
unloved progeny tiptoeing around the edges
of social acceptance

who is my protector
where is my protector
where … where … where

HUMANITY

HANGING OUT ON THE FRINGE

hanging out on the fringe
feeling alone in a
a world of
wars ... avarice ... injustice
unreasoning ... unquestionable conformists
sauntering about
like wooly... four-legged ones
lock stepping in a continuous rhythm
all directions the same

systems in reverse
blowing whistles ... alarming signals
be not afraid to stand alone
illusion of aloneness ... is but an illusion
be willing to represent

triggering realization in my solitude
bravery ... self-respect
opposed to prevailing directions
where all routes are the same

footsteps not embedded in the mire
holding on to my true self
soothingly calm awareness
embracing my acceptance
easterly winds dissipating fermented confusion

hanging out on the fringe
aglow with sparks brightening the path
allowing unexplored
radiance to burst forth.
accepting a fringe existence

EARTHQUAKE KATMANDU

inner earth core rumblings
colliding … shifting earth plates
releasing bass sounds
as the land shakes … shudders
offering no warnings … no places to escape

decimating … crumbling centuries old structures
vanishing in the flash of an idea
leaving mounds of sadness
holy shrines shaken from their ancient foundations
unable to offer solace to those seeking solutions

inhabitants circling themselves
lost in a sea of confusion
looking for possible survivors who may be buried
in depths to impossible to retrieve
relentlessly the clock of time lingers
oxygen flees

searching for meditative contemplation
monks and other holy ones consult their sources
for directions …   for guidance

singing birds … creatures large … small
looking for safer vistas beyond the obvious clutter
animal noises yield
leaving a sound void

the sky's continual radiance
hidden in dust … smoke and tears
reflections of the impermanence of this
earthly experience
as a mysterious force holds the reins of what's to come.

JUNETEENTH

... a national holiday has been proclaimed
giving recognition to the official ending
of the two-hundred-fifty -year stench
of slavery

private ... public institutions will close their doors
trees whose branches held the hanging ropes
release their leaves in homage to the bitter memories

brittle bones of slave escapees lingering at rivers' shores
reminiscent of encounters with poisonous reptiles
cries and shrieks as a last breath was released

male and female pickers
with darker skinned... parched... sun- burned bodies
forced to supply cotton for a wealth driven consciousness

1863 emancipation proclamation promised freedom
allowed sunshine's rays to offer relief to some
to others dark clouds of inferiority remained

two years later a general whose name was Granger
with soldiers into Galveston, Texas ...they rode
formally declaring the end of slavery

stench blown encounters were minimized
freedom … a righteous birth-right burst forth
affirmed by the freed ones

one-hundred fifty years later
the USA congress honors the slaves
acknowledges some injustices that became institutionalized

citizens as diverse as the vegetation breathe relief
descendants hold their heads high
flowers bloom … rains fall … winds blow
nineteenth day of June
gives national prominence
to those who sacrificed their breaths for a place in history
Juneteenth

URBAN STREETS

modern day Urban Streets
homeless man maneuvering his shopping cart
experiencing pangs of hunger
interrupting his cognitive flow
an obese … soft-bodied …
flesh eating omnivore passerby
with a vibrating stomach … complaining about digestion
wearing polished sneakers …

manicured trees
decimated into unreal perfect shrubs
whose relationship with nature has diminished
as winged creatures and crawling ones
search for friendlier habitats
in contrast to manufactured objects
from a plastic factory with no unique identity

pubescent un-chaperoned skateboarders
with their teenager peers
darting in and out of safety
scaling walls … jumping curbs
causing breaths to be suspended
as chests go hollow
exhibiting a false sense of daring
a mysterious power that separates
one from a solid foundation

those claiming a Goth type identity
black painted lips … black spiked hair
black leather boots … black pants
without knowledge of historical implications
walking in a serious rhythm

with a preordained destiny to
a place not welcoming the norm

boys with trousers below their derrieres
revealing an anal split
striding wide-legged to anchor a possible slippage
that would transport a coolness
into a confusing perplexing after thought
attempting to reveal their acceptance of
what ...where ... who

the resounding bedlam of horns
screeching tires bellowing sirens
signaling ones to the right
helicopters with their obnoxious unremitting clamor
directed by an infrastructure sanctioned by its populace
eliminating the possibility of calm

the Urban beat overpowers tranquility
with inhabitants blindly skimming the fringes
awaiting the coming of a new rescuer
who might save them from themselves
while they cling to un-manifested expectations
existing in the layers of deeply rooted gray matter

window shoppers gazing in awe
at goods beyond the reaches of their imaginations
shielding secret desires of ownership
yearning for jewels and satin
perfectly positioned away from the touches
of onlookers
mellifluous tones emanating from
church tower bells
alerting a populace of an unseen force
injecting momentary solace
into passersby going from point to point
urban streets

MY VISIT TO THE CITY OF THE ANGELS

my visit to the city of angels
being with myself
remembering … awaiting…. awaiting
blissful past-times when
notions of purity appeared accessible

what happened to blue skies
sequestered under a heavenly bordered smoggy brown haze
blocking the image of what used to be
endless visions of heaven's majesty

a visit to the city of the angels
citizens rushing about …minimum relaxation
churning … churning continuous agitation
brown hills … replacing green vegetation
dead and dry … no precipitation
scorched lawns burying possible sprouts
is the climate change causing the droughts

proselytizers on corners loudly preaching
sirens wailing… horns blowing …brakes screeching
anxious drivers speeding very fast
hoping each new moment won't be the last

from near and far away they are cunningly seduced
the alluring call … fame and glory has produced
breast implants … yoga … vegan … collagen supreme
orthodontically perfect smiles complete the dream
skinny ones …fat ones hoping to be discovered
muscular ones exhibiting fitness recently uncovered
promises of champagne and Russian caviar
one day they might become a movie star
if one has the fortitude and the right appeal
Hollywood future desires may become real

run-away teenagers who exited their domiciles
directions near and far from many miles
trying out newness wanting to be understood
rejecting their hurts awaiting something good
they roam during the nights ... sleep all day
hoping their lives will not whisk away
can L.A. offer any solution
despite dysfunctions and the pollution

downtown Los Angeles with edifices tall
dwellers in high-rises surrounding the mall
around a corner across the street
many citizens accepting defeat
their desire for comfort yet to be found
tied to the pavement they are bound
in boxes on the ground where some go to sleep
vermin ... defecation causing them to weep
beyond imagination homelessness grows
in other L.A. communities everything flows

police protect ... while carrying their gun
sending some folks in the hood on the run
the police helicopters circling around and around
unremittingly ...obnoxiously ... unwelcoming sound

crack ... crystal meth buyers and dealers selling
the edge of reason offers constant yelling
naked man standing on a corner complaining of heat
police fixated on a dead man lying under a sheet
some puzzled looking ... black men accepting defeat
allowing red lights...green lights to give them direction
confused in their lives with no refuge of protection
shopping carts filled to the extreme
pushed by those who have lost their dream
shoved by those looking for solutions
wanting gratifying conclusions

Rodeo Drive ... Melrose ... and Sunset Strip ...
where trends are designed for the very hip
Teslas glide by with much precision
erect sitting drivers ...a privileged decision
providing entry into a higher class
illusions ... illusions in time will pass

a day's heaviness the Santa Anas blow away
closing out the echo of a typical LA day
the clamor slowly withdraws from the freeway
carbon monoxide dissipates for a short duration
the breath receives available oxygen inhalation
helicopter's repetitive overtones freeze
auditory receptors vibrate with more ease

over the Pacific a most stunning evening sunset
with visions of renewal ... we must never forget
reminding one of an uncompromised beauty
respect to ourselves and nature ... it's our duty
a momentary pause ... a momentary relaxation
urban sprawl awaiting the new dawn in anticipation

ASPECTS OF MODERNITY

modernity and its fallout
exploitation of the earth for material gain
sacrificing the natural order with justification
willing to kill for constant control
decimated
cultures … forest … rivers
what am I honoring

looking at modernity and its fallout
as affluence becomes an overriding objective
alleged superior minds
justifying the need for more earthly rape
nullifying the brightness
overpowering those who live with earth's rhythms
in their simplistic daily routines
where majestic trees of green once kissed the clouds
are forced into splintering remains
what part do I play

as I look at modernity and its fallout
obliterating virginal places and paths
where
four legged ones have trod
crawling ones have slithered
attempting to remain untouched
under canopies of lace -feathered ferns
who… what am I… honoring

modernity and its fallout causes
salty flowing tears
from some older folks
attempting to understand a quickened contrast
yearning for pastime memories
simpler times more easily accessible
rainbows hanging out on the periphery of loveliness
pollinating bees insuring life's continuation
in my participation…
who … what am i honoring

in the midst of it all
observing pirouetting dancing clouds
returning blue skies
focusing on the fallout
I remind myself
modernity with its temporary concepts
is but another of the illusions

SEATTLE 5-STAR HOTEL

luxuriating in the splendor of a 5-star hotel
surrendering to the seduction of an oversized massage chair
indescribably satisfying those areas in need of attention
burying myself in the coziness of a goose-down comforter
conceding to pleasurable sensations
relaxing into the gift

viewing the sky whose dark foreboding clouds
have majestically and mysteriously been transformed into
dancing shapes morphing continuously
heaven's breath expels its liquid forces

from my vantage point observing
strollers with lighthearted gaits
wrapped in the creators' magnificent radiance
aware… unaware
of the subtleties … of the obvious
manifestations

oh… life is so good
a brief moment
the sun enters
through big transparent tinted glass windows
a temporary escape
into a fantastic comfort zone
where no thoughts of prevailing negativities
have permission to penetrate my psyche,

oh, life is so good

dark clouds have again returned
temporarily shielding the sun
a dance of retrospection
encumbering myself more deeply into
protective goose-down covers
shielding me from unwanted thoughts
burying myself in memories of the joy
that is accessible to all
viewing the blue sky in the distance
dark clouds … bright sun
two polarities
accenting the forever repetitive cycle of continuity

remembering darkness comes … light always reappears
and oh … how good life is
regenerating … recuperate… reenergizing
in the confines of a 5-star hotel in Seattle

WORLDWIDE NEWS RELEASE

NORTH ... SOUTH ... EAST ... WEST
what comes next
specific worshipers offer prostration
near bullets ... bombs continual frustration
eliminating hopes of future production
ideas frozen for positive construction
fighting ones ... escaping ones shouting ... running
avoid possibility of what's coming
along Gaza Strip blood shed becomes the norm
empathy for descendants yet to be born
painfully crying ... magnifying energy
deception ... destruction displacing synergy
conflicting ones proclaiming victory
ignoring truths regarding history
fear ... ignorance ... lies falsely succeed
intelligence ... solutions succumb to greed
uprooting the sweetness ... dates ... trees decay
preventing swaying fronds to freely sway

WEST.... NORTH .... EAST.... SOUTH
wondering what comes next
ignorance... stupidity... disrespected oceans
confuse the flow of the tides continuous motions
imbalance of remnants discarded plastic
creating a future ... possibly drastic
ruptured pipelines releasing oil
decimating sea-life ... even the soil
dead fishes and birds float on the sea
poisoned surfaces .... no places to flee
gasping and grasping and gasping and grasping

EAST… NORTH … SOUTH … WEST
wondering what comes next
fierce winds … dry hot sands constantly blow
sweltering sun an unbreathable flow
sunburnt leathery skin absorbing the heat
escaping immigrants with blistery feet
from places where shadows remain
saturated to the core with unyielding pain
unwelcoming deserts … snakes … scorpions abide
immigrants drowning … dying …no places to hide
cries for freedom the piercing call
automatic birthright should be for all
ancestors … ancestors on the alert
twenty first century still more hurt
ayudenos … ayudenos … ayudenos
sayidnee … sayidnee … sayidnee

SOUTH … NORTH … WEST… EAST
wondering what comes next
inner earth's explosive declarations
more powerful than all of the nations
discharged from earth's molten core
alert … there is always more
dormant volcanoes reawaken
nature's control often mistaken
emitting golden … glowing … flames of red
thoughts of the destruction that lies ahead
much in its path will surely die
smoke … blocking … blueness of the sky
notifying everyone … an un-stoppable force
so-called dormant volcano awakens … on its course
reminding habitants of an ethereal power
that can come and go at an undetermined hour

WEST…. NORTH…. SOUTH …. EAST
wondering what comes next
erupting pandemic … illusions of a vanishing sun
panic … ignorance … citizens on the run

masking up … accepting who knows what … spacing from others
confusion separating our sisters and our brothers
strong immunity and civility a necessary must
worldwide epidemic producing fear… distrust
lowly conscious ones with blurred selections
circling and circling with multiple directions
on jazmine scented paths where Asians once tread
spit upon …kicked until they bled
males … females … children and the old
scapegoated into a covid 19 victim's role
Asiatic ones received unjustified blame
racism … expletives … hate always the same

SOUTH…. WEST …. NORTH …. EAST
wondering what comes next
illusions of a drowning sun
waters here … water there
water … water … water everywhere
excessive rain overflowing dams

overflowing rivers … overflowing streams
diminishing … destroying some future dreams
uprooted trees … debris carving its path
nature reminds us of its possible rath

today's … yesterday's structures lost forever
a flash of time materials can sever
squealing … barking … howling animals going down river
this experience of nature is more than a shiver
anchored … unanchored barriers floating by
shouts and moans as people cry
hold on … hold on … hold on

EAST…. NORTH…. SOUTH…. WEST
wondering what comes next
illusion of a radiantly glowing sun
citizens on the run … what has been done
droughts depleting life's stability

more respect for earth's fragility
villages … towns … hot dry season returns
frightening reminders of past times burns
hearts and thoughts with moisture laden yearning
once green covered landscapes continuously burning
blowing winds create vortexes … ignite flames
transform … destroy… produce additional pains
rapidly moving mysteriously ignited fires
cancel the immediacy of future desires

NORTH …. WEST …. SOUTH …. EAST
wondering what comes next
piercing shrill thrown away sunshine
rapidly vanishing disappearing lifeline
I can't breathe … dissipating oxygen
rogue cops killing unarmed black men
will hate abate … I wonder when
under a canopy of low hanging clouds
mourners away from their tedium in black colored shrouds
with heads hanging low
tears in a directionless flow
no tomorrow becomes evident
where some lives are too quickly spent
lavish bouquets on caskets adorned
how many lives will still be mourned
the breath has gone away
a day's ending here to stay

SOUTH…. NORTH …. WEST …. EAST
what comes next
baffled illusions too severe
knowledge can make them disappear
stand sturdy do not flee
be the example you want to see
an acceptance of some perfection
a choice with well-defined selection
this amazing journey on the earth
promises unceasingly new birth

GANGS

Gangs were very prominent in the Los Angeles County area in 1997. A new experience was presented to me to work at county funded special school in Santa Monica, California. It was a school for school-age youth who had experienced a myriad of challenges and were not permitted to attend regular public schools. These young people were picked up each day and delivered back to their homes by a counselor.

I had an unusual experience the first day. Some of the boys wore their pants so low they exposed their anal split. The girls looked at me with much disdain and no degree of empathy. The students were new, but their particular challenges were familiar. I used my background in Theatre Arts to help them to find their voices and gain degrees of confidence and trust. I will never forget my experiences with these children. Here are the stories of three of them.

EPIPHANY IN THE SAN GABRIEL MOUNTAINS

One of my most outspoken, and extroverted students was Tyrone Wilson, tagged Short Dog. His height and untethered fierceness whenever he encountered rival gang members earned him that tag. His often- repeated mantra to his homies was: "I ain't got no fear of nothing or nobody." In the calmer, quieter, more sensitive settings when he was away from his gang a different personality revealed itself. Short Dog was an 18-year-old young man who demonstrated leadership qualities. One of my colleagues and I encouraged him-to attend "How to be a Man," a workshop held high up in the San Gabriel Mountains near L.A. That trip was the first time for him and many of the other young males from his area to escape the helicopters, sirens, and the constant din of a teeming city. Moments of tranquility and peace were ideas seen on television, Hollywood movies or read in some history books.

Goals of the workshop were to provide an opportunity for young males to explore themselves at deeper levels than they ever had; to question themselves in ways that allowed their vulnerability to step out of the dark recesses of those secret places; to commit more to their humanity; to erase the victimhood identity; to forgive themselves and others. The facilitator was Malidoma Patrice Some, the West African author and spiritual teacher.

Several days later after he had returned to the city, a family member was shot and killed by a rival gang. His "Homies" came to him with their weapons prepared to retaliate as would have been the previous response with much bloodshed and many tears. Because he was a respected leader of his gang Shoreline Crips (the name for black gang members who lived in areas west of central Los Angeles), he was able to persuade them to allow him to take their guns, an unprecedented action. Previously, options other than retaliation would not have been considered. With degrees of trepidation, the Homies obeyed his decision; however, doubts about his leadership emerged. Discarding weapons into the ocean polluting our environment was not an action I condoned, but for him it was a major life victory. He shared that he had never considered the possibility of resolving issues using methods other than violence.

Short Dog had been born into and lived a gang lifestyle. Both his parents had been rival gang members. Despite the high voltage he was exposed to, his mother and father in their limited, confused way offered him love. Perhaps, my student's strong sense of self was an inherited trait and one learned from living with two parents.

PAYBACK

Many gang members were in my classes, some mandated by court order. At a different school, I met a nineteen-year-old court ordered female student. Teresita

Gomez-had been separated from her family at age seven when they attempted to cross the United States border. T., as she was called, was an attractive young woman of average height with tattoos on both arms which included the names of her two

brothers, her mother and father. In communities where parental guidance is at times nonexistent, the gang-family supplies a dysfunctional need. The growth rate of gangs reflects the breakdown of a stable family structure, socioeconomic instability and the distrust of religion and spirituality. T had been adopted into a gang as a young girl and involved in much violence and sexual exploitation.

Teresita's options were to come to my classes or go to jail. According to the young woman, her gang, V13, supplied all her needs. They supplied food, drugs, companionship, and protection.

One day, entering class wearing unclean, baggy pants, and an oversized torn shirt, T was sweating and breathing rapidly. She reported one of her friends had been killed by a rival gang. My attempts to calm her down and suggest she might go to the restroom to adjust her appearance were ignored. Her behavior verified she was high. I did not inquire what she had ingested. She spoke rapidly with tears, Black mascara flowed down her cheeks. I attempted to calm her down, but nothing I offered had an impact. Many of her classmates also tried to soothe her pain, but it was too deep beneath the surface. It was unreachable.

She justified the need for retaliation and an obligation to "pay back." She expressed no emotion as she shared her story. "I did what had to be done," she said. When queried about the possibility of her imminent demise as a gang member, she

responded, "Everyone I have cared strongly for has been *offed,* or disappeared from my life, so when it's my turn, I will be okay, I am used to pain and suffering."

TODAY I'M NINE

Of the many stories I was privy to, at an elementary school, east of downtown Los Angeles, the most disturbing one was from a fourth-grade student in a gang-infested area.

I was confident about the lesson plan I had used successfully at different schools with the same age students in one of the more affluent areas. I assumed they were just children with social and economic differences. I was not prepared for the contrast. My

assignment for the students was to share what past or present events were important in their lives and why. Almost before I completed the lesson description, a young boy volunteered immediately. With very erect posture, and an air of superiority he walked to the front of the room, gave a clear delivery and a serious contribution.

The ~~very~~ troubling aspect was the fact that when his story was shared, his classmates smiled, laughed, or demonstrated no expression. My concern was, were they afraid, accepting, or numb because of the common occurrences that frequented their particular community? I was horrified at his sharing and very troubled. His report was not a joke, it appeared as if his nine-year-old birthday the next day would open new unexplored possibilities. A major transition was about to occur, a time to give honor to his maleness, an opportunity for acceptance from his peers and some older tormented gang members. In poetic form, I have shared his offering.

TODAY I AM NINE

Being in a gang…that's what I'll be
None of your rules and laws for me
Soon I get to leave this stupid school
won't prepare to be no puppet fool
boys with tats and clean white tees
pants and white socks stop at the knees
girls they be tough with teased sprayed hair
black painted lips … no one to care

I'm down
low riding shiny cars doing a drive by
hanging out day and night getting high
freeway chases we love to do
the cops freaking out chasing you
tagging on everybody's walls
carrying weapons into shopping malls
lots of nights in jail
nobody comes to pay bail

I'm down
being in a gang, I ain't got no fear
is my dream, cause my homies be near
I get to have my own gun
Lots of folks be on the run
Real soon I get to kill
That's the true fuckin deal

I'm down
Now is the right time
Everything's fine
Cause today I'm nine

RELEASE

A TRANSITION

a new dwelling
distances from fragrant … natural beauty of cascading wisteria
illumining my pathway with an electrifying significance
in faraway realms of my consciousness
like the continual movement of shape-shifting clouds
paralleling my forward direction
changing … growing … evolving

the juxtaposition of self-worth
an inspiringly … surprisingly
sometimes sad awareness
appearing beyond my reach
touching unexplored realms in my unfolding
observing … awaiting solutions
penetrating surfaces of my awareness
searching for more soothing transitions

a gradual inhalation …a soothing exhalation
a satisfying gratitude … a miniscule reality
a loving unfolding of a magnificent quest
manifesting within my grasp

songbirds and coqui frogs chanting melodies
penetrating deeply into my soul
strengthening my understanding of
unfulfilled desires that have since vanished
where glorious solutions have appeared

OH SWEET SLUMBER

lying in bed welcoming slumber that's evading my wanting
begging relief from exhausted memories of a day's journey
the body's continual output in need of pause
as night fades into a new dawning where sunrise awaits

do not abandon me
in my need for regeneration
my desire for deep all encumbering sleep
as I recline under a brilliant canopy
the evening sky's celestial .... magnificent brilliance
displaying comets and constellations traversing
to distances beyond my knowing

do not sever our connection
as my body contracts
as my senses call out
as my discomfort magnifies
as I await your embrace to soothe my longings
releasing me from anxiety
hindering my receptivity

caressing my being ... fulfilling my desire
that I may relax into the present
where my need for your acceptance
outweighs the mental gyrations
I welcome the connection
where peace and tranquility abide

on this moonless night
observing the external movements of the day
I am alerted to the fleeting moments
as my body cries out return ... return ...return ...
Oh sweet slumber

Fifty-seven years of marriage...........
Another sleepless night as I cared for my ailing husband.

A BREATHLESS ENCOUNTER OF THE COSMOS

On a moonless desert night
where the visual expanse is outside definition
an eerie quietness interrupted by a distant howl
looking for answers.... maybe questions
movement in all directions
beyond simple explanations
the sky provides a lightshow of
glistening … streaking … glowing
moving … vanishing … appearing objects
trajectory beyond my earthy vision
too grand for simple minds comprehension

magnificent heavenly display
mysterious unraveling in this majestic overview
stars of undefinable sizes close and farther away
than eyes can explain
than feelings can express
dancing streaks of lights
distances beyond constellations
rapidly beating heart
churning inners…sweat dripping

glorious awareness unleashing
breath defying encounter
with whom … with what
definitions revoked
explanations cancelled
touching the surface of a different dimension
past … present … future collide
in an effort for more clarity
pausing … listening … surrendering
awaiting a better understanding of the unknown
on this quiet … warm … cloudless
almost surreal desert night

THE PASSING

as the winds continuously repattern the obvious
my realization alerts me to the acceptable clutter
which presents an illusion of permanence
while searching for that which provides resolutions

a finality that is in question
as I probe the infinite night sky
where the illusion of completeness
is for those on a dimly lit trajectory

the unfolding this life of mine has accessed
deep soulful connection
offering harmonious clarification
loving stimulation
perfectly penetrating the soul
as the breath surrenders

WHERE DID YOU GO

your last breath and darkness
or was it light
into a new dawn
with vistas too bright
for earthly explanations
or a new beginning
into an unexplored realm
voiceless domains
whose dimensions challenge novices
with a splendid grandeur
not explainable with ordinary verbiage
where did you go

HAWAII

VIEW FROM AN UPCOUNTRY WINDOW

In the early morn up country on Maui
wind dances its way across the spaces
well-defined movements
blowing away sluggishness and chaos in the atmosphere
sparkling environment … newly found crispness …
as if
directed by a seasoned choreographer.
a windless day at the seashore
calmness prevails offering a lake-like stillness
the absence of constant white caps
the mighty Pacific gently ebbing and flowing
displaying a cobalt blue exterior with hints of turquoise
another Maui day has begun

gentleness … tranquility step forth
I scan other directions
bold clouds frequently displaying their dark grey covers
presiding over the tops of Iao Valley have vacated
witnessing the newness of the day
breathing into the acceptance of unexplored possibilities.

Gratefully becoming suspended
into the thoughts of the magnificence
I absorb from this view
reminded of yesterday's fractures … tomorrow's chasms
having no place in this prevailing presence
The NOW is ever more evident
surrendering to the majesty of the moment
showering myself with awesome radiance.
surveying the new day
rhythmically moving winds
keeping in perfect harmony
with the rotational movement of the earth
blossoming flowers … chirping birds … smiling babies
surrendering to joy
as I view the valley below from my upcountry
Maui bedroom window

PELE

Dynamic hot embers
Ignited deep from within earth's center
Emitting electrifying golden crimson rage
Erupting high in the sky
Brighter than July's fourth

More fury than tumultuous seas
Agitated by shifting earthly contractions
Releasing plumes of noxious gases
Obstructing heavenly views
Commanding attention of the populace
With their involuntary sneezes......burning eyes

Molten lava cascading downward
Carving a deliberate path into the sea
Where Marine life flee
Expanding landmass beyond view
Offering flora and fauna brand new
reminder of what holds the power
each moment now and every hour

creating new
Poho'e ho'e......................A'a
Fresh ohia, fragrant lehua

Emerging, destroying, expanding
Exploding, creating, being Pele

Pele is the name of the Hawaiian volcano deity who creates volcanic landscapes

SATURDAY MORNING IN MAKAWAO

pale leg tourists supporting bloated bellies
donning matching attire
cameras strung around necks bouncing against breast
wide-eyed vacationers strolling Baldwin Avenue
under a heavily shrouded cloud covered sky
attempting to escape the inclement weather
of their faraway abodes
across the ocean's multi-directional expanse

an intermittent blue heaven reveals shape-shifting clouds
gracefully holding on to a direction
hovering a sprinkling precipitation
arched by rainbows reminiscent
of the eternal dance of sunlight

shops exteriors suggestive of past times
eroding oxidized structures and figurines
give pause to onlookers whose thoughts are pierced
upon entrance to a modern day shabby-chic environment
imported and domestic goods displayed by shop owners

wide-eyed curious tourists with puzzled expressions
pause as a Makawao hen with cackling progeny
immerge in unison searching for tasty morsels
depositing their evacuation in the pathways
of newly purchased vacation footwear
obstructing the visitor's gaits

sunshine enters Makawao
rain clouds drift to distant directions
holding their precipitation
tourists breathe a sigh of astonishment
a rainbow sky brightens the morning
Makawao welcomes the evolving new day
as visitors inhale…exhale and honor the splendor

HAWAIIAN TOURISTS

recently arrived tourists
strapped in newly rented convertibles
tops down … wind-blown hair
traversing in a Hana direction

intensity of the sun's solar rays
forces non-acclimated visitors
to apply toxic sea life poisoning sunscreen
while perfectly blowing Maui trade winds
caressing the environment releasing salty breezes.

recently arrived tourists
looking for escapes from familiar surroundings
descend on Maui where micro-climates prevail
dissipating… regenerating … sharing precipitation

convertible tops are raised and lowered
intense hues give vibrancy to
rainbows illumining the sky
mountain- tops peering through dancing cloud-covers
moving in directions far and near

recently arrived tourists
breathing in Maui air
tunneling through a road lined with
mango groves…bamboo forests… waterfalls … endless ocean vistas
sending a reenergized life force
to atrophied cells awaiting newness
allowing for reflective moments
as imaginations
touch the surfaces of reality
beyond a curve in the road where Hana awaits

SHADOW OF HALEAKALA

and in the shadows of Haleakala
the Nene habituates
songbirds chant harmonious melodies
a forest of eucalypti sway in unison
endangered Koa anchor their roots deeply
attempting to hold on

and in the shadows of Haleakala
winds from prescribed directions
blow away stagnant thought forms
that can prevent the metamorphosis
of freshness from having its day

and in the shadows of Haleakala
occasional axis deer leap across
a perfectly choreographed route
while travelers marvel at the grace
and hunters pause in readiness

and in the shadows of Haleakala
unprecedented vistas on cloudless days
reveal a valley of sugar cane
where mongoose and others reside
and profound secrets hide

and in the shadows of Haleakala
the day dims as a silvery silent
gray patch of shape-shifting clouds
deposit moisture
obscuring views
of the constantly changing pacific

and in the shadows of Haleakala
the majestic lao citadels
shrouded in a misty haze cloud cover

perfectly carved landscape
pristine liquid tributary
offering places of respite
to those seeking refuge

and in the shadows of Haleakala
sit and ponder questions
under an infinitely blue sky
stillness signals my patience
alerting a tranquility
as windblown answers silently reveal
a universal acceptance of all there is

MAUNA LOA

volcanic haze
shields the sky's blueness
soaring feathered friends
anchored to tree branches
awaiting the return of westerly bound breezes
rapidly beating hearts
longing for calmer rhythms

volcanic dust
a reminder of an invisible power
burning eyes … minimized oxygen
choking lungs
awaiting cleansing trade winds to blow away
disturbances emitted from Mauna Loa's core

volcanic pollution
an illusion of low clinging clouds
biological processes slow down
propelling … driving …releasing
carbon monoxide
adding to the discordant flow
offering no solutions while
expecting immediate relief

\

volcanic emissions
confusing those in its midst
with its insidious haze
similar to urban smog
offering no visual objectivity

volcanic disturbances
sending out warnings
for those who dare to
reject the possibilities
of nature's invisible powers

volcanic eruptions
ejaculating bright ... reddish ... orange ... hot ... destructive lava
incendiary warnings
melting away visions disturbing the calm
abolishing habitats ... increasing the landscape ...
providing a reminder
of nature's incredibly ... magnificently mysterious power

COMPLETION

IMAGINE A NEW PARADIGM

smiles shared … beauty beyond definition … vanishing desires
equality… essentials … justice for all BEINGS
peaceable winds saturating the surroundings
purity minimizing disharmony
fading into irretrievable realms
echoing frequencies … alerting citizens
love is possible

individuals rushing about with the rapidity
of hurricanes
attempting to feel complete
collide into a reality that
slows the tempo

imagine a new paradigm
murky mind thoughts
embedded deeply as impenetrable canyons
blocking visibility
release their corrosive hold
wash away in streams of forgiveness
allowing emerging endless possibilities

children's unrestrained laughter encircling
the atmosphere with melodious harmonies
blocking foggy discord
signaling a sweet breeze brushed … transparent reality
exemplifying a purity of hearts

anxiety halted
beautifully… affirming … aroused awakenings
people coming together… celebrating Oneness
benevolence permeates beyond perception
breath pausing moments
breathe in … inhale the radiance
imagine a new paradigm

THANKFUL

thankful I am
for the sweetness of the songbirds
whose chants recap the available purity
beautiful never-ending reminders
enveloping the spaces

so grateful am I
as the slice of a new day peeking through a
misty fog filled morning lifting away
into the promise of a sunny day
with gliding clouds providing that which they do

thankful am I
accepting the stillness
listening to whispers into my consciousness
guiding me to more hopeful paths
diminishing obstacles
dazzling lights illuming my path

so much to be thankful for
daily reflections morphing into
an annual remembrance
providing hope

color changing leaves fall to the ground
fertilizing the earth for newness to emerge
transitory nature of existence
regeneration ... sleeping cells reignite

goodness and delight available to all
falling rain ... sky-filled rainbows
outpourings of laughter ... uncontrollable joy escaping
tiptoeing on the fringe of the remarkable
running...shouting children
demonstrating freedom
available abundance ... gifts of love ... friendships
I get to share and receive
for these and so much more I am thankful
oh yes

PIECE OF PERFECTION

an intrinsic part of the universe
I am…we are
tears as salty as seas that wash the shores
the same
as kings … queens … remembered ones … forgotten ones

inhabitants of this planet
with personalities as dark as a moonless night
or
as bright as the sparkling sunshine on a snowy day

as diverse … as varied as
multicolored flowers
displaying their varieties

our different tones … hues … shades of skin
sometimes close entrances … sometimes open exits

many are ignored as first-class citizens
to some of life's possibilities
different beliefs we have
different directions we go

some are treated as if they are invisible
invisibility is but a fantasy
the true essence shrouded in a web of uncertainty

each of us a part of life's puzzle
together we bind the pieces
I am you …you are me.
I am an on-purpose piece of perfection as are you

And so it is...

Gratitude … appreciation to those who offered support
and patience as I created
A PIECE OF PERFECTION

Maui Poets Society
Waimea Writer's -Tutu's House
Hilo Writers Group
Hawaii Writer's Guild
Hawaii Writer's Alliance
Channa Grace
Pamela Wai'olena
Owen's Family
Richard Coleman Jr.
Mesiyah Mc Ginnis
Rickie Byars / Greta Sesheta Soul Sister's Retreat
Jan Williamson, 18th Street Arts Complex
My Children: Carter, Gentry, Sunny, Tagi
My Grandchildren: Cheayenne, Karimah,Elias
Sekaya, Orion, Jonothan
My great-grandchild: Sofina

THE POET

Gwyndolin Gorg grew up in Los Angeles, California. She has worked professionally for more than fifty years as an actress, model, dancer, singer, songwriter, storyteller, producer, director, educator, and theatre manager.

She served as the educational coordinator of the 18th Street Arts Complex in Santa Monica. The California Arts Council awarded Ms. Gorg a grant to produce a documentary showing relationships between teenagers and senior citizens. In 2007, she was honored as teacher of the year by the United Teachers of Los Angeles. At the International House of Blues Foundation, Hollywood, she co-created their Blues Schoolhouse Program as a performing artist and a history consultant. She studied at the Los Angeles Theatre Academy with Jeff Corey, James Whitmore, Ricardo Montalban and Francine Parker, with a request performance for Paul Robeson. Ms. Gorg co-founded the Hilo Theater for Youth. She was appointed resident Artist in the Schools by the Hawaii State Department of Education. At Leeward College, she wrote, produced, directed, and hosted the *Oahu Gazette*, a community television magazine show. She wrote and produced the Documentary, *Inside State Prison,* about Oahu Penitentiary, winner of the Special Honors at the Los Angeles International Film exhibition (Filmex).

Ms. Gorg's film credits include writing and producing *Autobiography of A Hopi* American Indian history and traditional values. She wrote and produced *The Savages* an award winning educational documentary *on* street gangs, recently restored at UCLA's film and archive division. Her entertainment feature film writing and producing credits include *Living the Blues*, starring the legendary Sam Taylor, winner of a Filmtrax award at the Ghent International Film Festival in Belgium for its outstanding presentation of musical culture and a Best Feature Nomination at the American Film Institute Video Awards. Ms. Gorg has written *I Am The Blues*, a children's book published by Pacific Raven Press in twenty- one languages; *Nice Lady a lighter approach to Alzheimer's*; *I Am Bigger Than Nigger*; and *Darlene's Awakening*.
She and her husband met and married three weeks later while serving in the Civil Rights movement. They remained married for 57 years until his demise in 2020. She makes her home in Hawaii with her children and grandchildren.

www.ingramcontent.com/pod-product-compliance
Lightning Source LLC
Chambersburg PA
CBHW062112090426
42741CB00016B/3396